Summary of

All the Light We Cannot See

by Anthony Doerr

Instaread

Please Note

This is a summary and analysis.

Table of Contents

Summary

The lives of two teens, a French girl and a German boy, improbably intersect at the end of World War II in *All The Light We Cannot See.*

Before the war, Marie-Laure LeBlanc, who has been blind since childhood, lives comfortably in Paris with her father, Daniel, who is the key master for the natural history museum. She loves to visit the museum and learn, especially about molluscs, or snails. Her father makes her a detailed wooden replica of their neighborhood so she can learn to navigate it. He also makes complicated wooden puzzle boxes that delight her. He gives her a Braille copy of Jules Verne's *Around the World in Eighty Days* and then, after she devours it, the first volume of *Twenty Thousand Leagues Under the Sea.* Marie-Laure is also fascinated by a story she hears at the museum of a fabulous diamond hidden there, called the Sea of Flames. The diamond is said to make its owner immortal, but curse the owner's loved ones.

Werner Pfennig lives in a threadbare orphanage in a drab mining town in Germany. Frau Elena, who runs the orphanage, is kind, though the place is threadbare. Werner is close to his little sister, Jutta, who dreams of going to Paris and draws pictures of what she imagines it must look like. Werner finds and fixes up a discarded radio for the orphanage. Werner and Jutta are mesmerized by a radio program about science for children that they hear on the radio. Soon Werner's repair services are in demand in the neighborhood. Werner is praised and treated to cream cakes when he fixes the mine supervisor's radio, then sent to an elite Nazi school because of his mechanical ability.

An angry Jutta warns Werner about the Nazis and their brutishness, but the townspeople treat him as a hero. At first, he believes he is living up to an ideal of glorious service to the Fatherland and Hitler's plan to cleanse the world. At the school, Schulpforta, the teachers are harsh, especially with boys who cannot keep up with the physically and mentally demanding training. Werner is singled out by science teacher, Dr. Hauptmann, for his skill with radios and put to work on a special project involving triangulation of signals. He befriends Frederick, a slight, dreamy boy who loves birds and is bullied by the brutal commandant, Bastian. Frederick invites Werner to his home in Berlin. It is the most luxurious place Werner has ever seen, though Frederick's mother says they will get an even better flat when a neighbor, an old Jewish woman, is removed. At school, Frederick receives even more abuse from teachers and students despite his family's status. Werner does not interfere in the bullying, but he does attempt to help Frederick in other, small ways, such as polishing his boots for him. Frederick is beaten so badly that he is brain-damaged and sent home. Werner is dismayed when he visits him in Berlin again.

As Germany invades, Marie-Laure and Daniel flee Paris. Daniel has been given one of four Sea of Flames, three of which are copies and one is the real thing. Neither Daniel nor the three other people given the stones know which is the real one. This is done in an effort to keep the precious stone out of Nazi hands. Daniel and Marie-Laure walk for two days to reach Evreux, where Daniel is to contact a museum official, but the man is gone. They hitch a ride toward the citadel city of Saint-Malo on the Atlantic coast, where Daniel's uncle, Etienne, lives.

Etienne recorded a radio show on science for children with his brother before World War I. However, during the war, Etienne's brother was killed. Due to his grief, Etienne has become a recluse, living only with his housekeeper, Madame Manec. Etienne and Madame happily welcome Marie-Laure and Daniel into their home. Not long afterward, the Germans invade Saint-Malo.

Advised of Marie-Laure's fascination with molluscs, a friend of Madame's shows Marie-Laure an abandoned kennel in a grotto filled with snails. She is given a key to the grotto so she can visit whenever she likes. She visits often.

A Nazi gemologist, Sergeant Major von Rumpel, is hunting the Sea of Flames. He finds and assesses pilfered treasures, avoiding any thoughts of how they were obtained. He has tumors in his throat and hopes that the Sea of Flames can cure him. By threatening museum officials, he learns the names of the four people given the diamonds. After successive disappointments, he hones in on Daniel.

Daniel hides the Sea of Flames in a tiny model of Etienne's house when he builds a miniature Saint-Malo so that Marie-Laure might use it to learn how to navigate the unfamiliar streets. In December of 1940, he receives a telegram ordering him back to the museum in Paris. He is arrested when he is found with skeleton keys and drawings of Saint-Malo. He is charged with plotting to blow up Saint-Malo based on information from Claude Levitte, the local butcher. Levitte provided German officials with pictures of Daniel taking measurements of the city. Daniel is sent to a labor camp in Germany. When he writes to Marie-Laure, he lies about the treatment he receives in the labor camp. Eventually, the letters stop.

As the Germans tighten their hold over Saint-Malo, Madame organizes a mini-resistance. She and her lady friends sabotage the Nazis, beginning with small things like losing the mail, but eventually moving to larger things, like transmitting secret codes to the Allies. Madame asks Etienne to help with this using the transmitter he and his brother used to transmit their science program, but he refuses until Madame becomes ill and dies. As Marie-Laure brings the codes home from the bakery where they have been baked into special loafs of bread, Etienne broadcasts them. The transceiver is hidden in the attic where a large wardrobe with a hole cut in the back for entry blocks the door.

Werner begins to see that Jutta is right about the Nazis. He asks Hauptmann to send him home. Instead, though Werner's design for triangulation equipment has won Hauptmann a promotion to Berlin, Hauptmann sends him to the eastern front. Hauptmann feels Werner is getting too much attention for his designs. Werner is just fifteen, though he is told that Hauptmann has learned that he is really eighteen. His squad leader is Volkheimer, a giant of a boy who was ahead of him at school and helped test the triangulation project. With the equipment Werner designed, their squad combs the countryside for illegal radio transmissions and kills anyone found near them. In one mission they mistakenly kill a mother and a sweet-looking little girl. The girl's death haunts Werner.

After many brutal missions in 1943 and 1944, Werner's team goes to Saint-Malo to look for the transceiver sending out number codes. Von Rumpel also arrives in Saint-Malo. He accosts Marie-Laure at the grotto. She can hear that he has a limp. She tells him Daniel left her nothing of value. He leaves, at least for the moment. She finds the stone in the tiny house and ponders returning it to the sea.

Saint-Malo becomes a final Nazi holdout against the advancing Allies. Werner locates the source of the broadcasts but does not turn Etienne in because he recognizes his voice. He is the radio science professor from his childhood.

Bombs rain on the town. The hotel where Werner and Volkheimer are working is destroyed and they are buried in the cellar by debris. Werner gets a radio going and hears Marie-Laure broadcasting. Etienne has been interned by the Nazis and she is alone. She hears the limping man enter the house. She hides in the attic and begs for help on the radio. Werner tells Volkheimer about her and he agrees that Werner should try to help. Though it is risky, Volkheimer uses grenades to blow a hole in the debris. Werner rushes to Etienne's house. He surprises von Rumpel near the hidden attic door and shoots him in a struggle.

Marie-Laure emerges. They learn of their connection through the radio science professor. They share a can of peaches, her last food. Werner thinks he may be in love, but tells her they must part because she will be safer without him. She takes him to the grotto, where she throws the tiny wooden house into the water. She asks how he will find her again. He does not know. She slips something into his hand. After she is gone, he finds the grotto key.

The Allies take the town. Marie-Laure reunites with Etienne. Werner is captured. He suffers a flare-up of a dysentery-like illness. Disoriented, he wanders off from a hospital tent and dies when he steps on a landmine. Jutta is told of the circumstances of his death. Along with Frau Elena and the last few girls at the orphanage, she was ordered to Berlin to work in a factory. Soviet soldiers find them and rape them.

Marie-Laure and Etienne make a new life in Daniel's Paris flat. They never learn all the details of Daniel's death. Marie-Laure finishes her education and becomes a renowned expert on mollusks. She has a daughter, Helene, from a friendly, but not serious relationship. Eventually, she also has a grandson.

Jutta becomes a math teacher, marries and has a son. In 1974, Volkheimer, who is now a TV antenna repairman, is asked to identify Werner's personal items. When he does, he requests that he be allowed to take them to

Jutta. Inside Werner's bag, Jutta finds the tiny replica of Etienne's house and tracks it to the real one in Saint-Malo. A neighbor helps her locate Marie-Laure. Jutta goes to Paris in search of Marie-Laure, also satisfying her childhood dream of seeing Paris. She brings along her young son, a boy much like Werner. She gives the box to Marie-Laure. Inside is the iron key to the grotto, suggesting to Marie-Laure that Werner rescued the wooden house from the sea, but the Sea of Flames is no longer there.

Main Characters

Marie-Laure LeBlanc: Marie-Laure, a bright, curious Parisian girl, goes blind at the age of six. She loves snails, puzzles and books by Jules Verne.

Daniel LeBlanc: Daniel is Marie-Laure's widowed father. He is the key master and locksmith for the Paris natural history museum.

Werner Pfennig: Werner, a German orphan, is selected for Schulpforta, a Nazi political school where he becomes a radio expert. He is sent to the eastern front at the age of fifteen to locate and destroy enemy radio transmissions.

Jutta Pfennig: Jutta is two years younger than her brother Werner, but she is his moral compass because of her strong sense of right and wrong. She loves to draw pictures of what she imagines Paris looks like.

Etienne LeBlanc: Etienne, Daniel's uncle, lives in the family home in Saint-Malo and has not come out since the World War I when his beloved brother died.

Madame Manec: Madame is Etienne's housekeeper. She becomes active in the resistance.

Frederick: Frederick, Werner's friend at school, is a small, fragile boy and a bird lover. He is singled out and abused at school.

Frank Volkheimer: Volkheimer, an older student, is feared by the boys because he is large. He later becomes Werner's sergeant.

Reinhard von Rumpel: Von Rumpel, a sergeant major, is a Nazi treasure hunter. Von Rumpel wants to find the Sea of Flames because he believes it can heal tumors in his throat.

Thank you for purchasing this Instaread book

**Download the Instaread mobile app to get
unlimited text & audio summaries
of bestselling books.**

Visit Instaread.co
to learn more.

Analysis

Character Relationships

Though Marie-Laure and Werner are the main characters, they do not meet until near the end of *All the Light We Cannot See*. To understand them, and the people they interact with along the way, the reader needs only to answer the questions implied by the novel's title.

Marie-Laure and Werner

In terms of vision, Marie-Laure and Werner are opposite sides of the same coin. Though she is blind, she remains pure and innocent because she can see with her heart. Her very name reflects this. Her first name comes from the Virgin Mary, who is associated with goodness and light, and her last name, LeBlanc, means the white, another association with goodness. Marie-Laure tries always to keep up the spirits of those around her. Of course, she has not known penury or abandonment, as Werner has. She is loved and cherished first by her father, then by Etienne and Madame. Etienne sees in her glow the meaning of life. Her soul is so pure and good that people, even strangers, naturally want to help her. As Dr. Geffard at the museum reflects, just to see her makes people feel that goodness cannot be extinguished.

Conversely, Werner has perfect eyesight but cannot see the truth until it is too late for him. He loses his innocence, and almost his soul. His orphaned childhood is a hard one. His last name is the essence of ordinary. A pfennig is a common, small coin. Unlike Marie-Laure, he has no father or uncle to love or guide him, only a little sister who needs him to guide her. Their father died in a coal mine, and a despondent Werner is told repeatedly that the mines are where he is going, too. When Werner gets a chance to apply his mechanical aptitude, and make himself a place in the great machine of Germany, he grabs it, shoving aside his sister's warning about Nazi atrocities. When he attends the elite Nazi school, however, he begins to see their brutality, racism and sadism, but cannot bring himself to help his bullied friend, Frederick. It is too late for him. He ends up on the deadly eastern front, where he is shattered by endless, senseless killing, especially after his team murders a little girl. He saw the girl playing earlier, and she became for him an emblem of the idea that goodness still exists. By the time he gets to Saint-Malo, Werner has seen so much evil that he is haunted by it constantly. It takes Marie-Laure's light to get him to finally step up for what he knows to be right. He can literally see the goodness and purity in silver light that illuminates her. When he rescues her, he knows that he has done a good thing at last even if he is broken. He wonders whether they could have had a future together, but tells her they must separate because being with him is unsafe for her. Literally, he means that being with a German soldier is dangerous, but in a broader sense, he sees that he is too damaged and contaminated to be with her. He then becomes ill and disoriented, causing him to wander away from an American hospital tent and onto a landmine. The death is an accident, yet perhaps it is a subconscious reaction of his crushed soul, seeking an exit. Just as Marie-Laure always carries light with her, he has become, especially to himself, a figure of darkness.

Madame Manec

Madame Manec is also an important representational character. She has an indomitable French elegance even in wartime. A true French cook, she can make a magnificent meal from the poorest of rations. She tries, at first, to stay out of the Nazis' way when they occupy her town, but she is too much of a patriot to continue to do nothing. She organizes her lady friends and eventually pulls the reluctant Etienne into the resistance as well. In all this, she becomes an emblem of her beloved France in the same way Werner represents Germans who went along with the Nazi program because they were indoctrinated or wanted to get ahead. Madame literally sees everything, down to the smallest blade of grass, and has a clear vision of right, wrong, and the power of love to make a brighter future.

Character Counterpoints

Madame and Werner have their own counterpoints as well. Madame's opposite number is the sleazy butcher, Claude Levitte, who cozies up to the Nazis for material benefit and informs on Daniel. He is the epitome of collaboration at its worst. He even smells rotten. Von Rumpel, too, is an opposite reflection of Madame's heart and bravery. The Nazi treasure hunter does what he is told, believing he is just an average man who will eventually go home to his wife, kids and normal job. He can forget what he has been a part of. He refuses to see the truth of where the treasures he evaluates, the jewelry and paintings, have come from. His illness symbolizes this. His soul is being eaten away by what he is doing.

Werner's opposites among German youth are both Jutta and Frederick. Jutta, wise beyond her years, worries over the treatment of a Jewish classmate and the confiscation of Werner's electronics book simply because a Jew wrote it. She is distraught as she sees Werner fall for the Nazi rhetoric. Jutta has no way to escape the Nazis, as she is forced to labor for them, but her vision stays clear. Though she is raped by Russian soldiers, she is able to build a new life for herself and raise a beautiful, undamaged son who shines as brightly as Werner once did.

Frederick, Werner's school friend, has no such happy ending. Though he needed thick glasses, he could see what was true. Amid brutality and propaganda, he kept his eyes on the stars and the birds that he loved, birds he saw as symbols of freedom. The most brutish of the boys at the school killed birds just for fun, and this, rather than the treatment shown him personally, upset Frederick. Yet there were always more birds. Like the stars, and like the dream of freedom, they could not be extinguished. This vision buoyed Frederick. Even as he was beaten, he kept his eyes on the sky. He saw clearly that one must put others first, and was unafraid to refuse orders to torture a near-dead prisoner that had come to the school after he was caught stealing from a nearby farmhouse. The students were instructed to pour water on him in freezing temperatures. Frederick was the only one to refuse. Frederick's beautiful mind being so badly damaged is an enormous loss.

Themes

Loss

The theme of loss is a major one in *All the Things We Cannot See*, which takes such a stark look at war and what it does to people, especially children. Few young people, faced with terror and indoctrination, can separate what they are told is right from what is truly right, as Jutta does, or keep their innocence, as Marie-Laure does. Though Marie-Laure and Jutta are saved, Werner, and Frederick, as well as everything they might have been, are lost. Even Volkheimer, who is forever changed by all he experienced in the war, can be counted as a loss.

This sweeping sense of loss, however, finds balance in its counterpart, as voiced by Madame and embodied by Marie-Laure. That counterpart is the fact that love and goodness will endure. There is no clear answer as to why, and this is another major point of the novel. For some people, such as Madame, it is a matter of faith. For others, such as Daniel and Etienne, both men of science, it is one of the many puzzles that make up life. To solve them is the challenge and joy of living. Puzzles are, in fact, one of the most prevalent images in *All the Light We Cannot See*, from the wooden puzzle boxes that Daniel makes for his daughter to solve to the very existence of wars and inhumanity. Some of these puzzles have answers, some do not. They may be beyond human understanding, but life goes on. It takes bravery to live life fully, as do Marie-Laure and Madame, and as Etienne learns to do from their example, but it can be done. When Etienne finally agrees to help the resistance, he realizes that he was not living until that moment.

The Disasters of War

In order to really understand these characters, readers must fully grasp the realities of what it was like during World War II in Europe. Anthony Doerr builds up a fully realized portrayal of that terrible time, from the daily awfulness of available food, to the fear of being arrested or killed by a bomb at any time, to the blood-curdling inhumanity of the Schulpforta indoctrination school to, finally, the horrific murders perpetrated by Werner and his team in Eastern Europe. By the time Werner goes to the eastern front, finding a hard-boiled egg to eat becomes almost a holy experiment. In Saint-Malo, Marie-Laure is lucky when she can get some coarse bread. Everywhere people are so hungry that they are eating pets and birds off the street. People run out of fuel, too, and must burn anything they can find, as Marie and Etienne do. At school, Werner muses that they are even running out of boys to fuel the war. Daniel gets picked up by the authorities and disappears. Etienne avoids this same fate only because the war ends. This is the context of daily life in which the story must be placed.

For those in the military, or military schools, the situation is much worse. The game that the teachers lead at Schulpforta, who is the weakest, shows how easily adults can turn children into killers in these conditions. This is reinforced, graphically, when the boys must take turns torturing a near-dead prisoner who is staked out in the schoolyard. That is not enough of an example for these indoctrinators of children. The body of this man, who is explained away as less than human because he is not German, is left out to rot, fodder for carrion crows. By the time Werner goes back to Berlin to see Frederick after he is nearly beaten to death, Werner's stress is so great that he sees the mannequins in store windows as corpses. This stress grows during his killing missions, as he hallucinates Jutta surrounded by dead babies and a dead little girl coming out of the sky to chase him. Volkheimer, too, though he is older and stronger, is destroyed by his experiences. This is the anguish of those forced to endure the horrors of war, magnified because they are so young. That life goes on become both a miracle and a puzzle.

A Puzzlement

Puzzles, large and small, underline the central message of life as a mystery. Daniel makes elaborate puzzle boxes that Marie-Laure delights in solving. She is also fascinated by the spiraled structure of the nautilus, which is like a puzzle box. The world of the streets around her, in her blindness, is a less delightful puzzle, but she learns bravery as she uses the models of Paris and Saint-Malo to learn to get around by herself. When she gets to Etienne's house, she finds it constructed like a puzzle, but she knows how to master it. She is ready when she is needed to pick up coded messages at the bakery and bring them home for Etienne to transmit for the resistance. For Werner, science, and especially radio waves, are the puzzles that intrigue him and give him joy when he solves them.

The Sea of Flames diamond and its myth present one of the grand puzzles of the novel. Its very existence is a rumor to all but a few high-ranking museum officials, and it is cleverly hidden by a puzzle-like series of safes, boxes, and locks. There is a myth that the diamond offers its owner immortality while cursing the owner's loved ones. Daniel does not believe in this myth. For him, everything can be explained by either chance or physics. He has the diamond only briefly, but is arrested and sent to a work camp as soon as he turns it over to Marie-Laure's keeping, though she does not realize she has it until much later. Before it is thrown into the sea, Daniel dies a prisoner, Madame gets pneumonia and dies, and Etienne is arrested. Marie-Laure, though, miraculously survives the bombardment that destroys Etienne's house around her, and escapes von Rumpel. Maybe this is a coincidence, but maybe not. Each person must find his or her own answer to the riddle of the stone. A final chapter dedicated to the Sea of Flames suggests that it is waiting on the seafloor for a chance to do more mischief, whether that is through powers of magic or just the power of suggestion is yet another puzzle. The human brain, as Etienne muses, remains the greatest puzzle, creating mazes of good and evil, light and dark. The Sea of Flames conundrum is one of them.

Light and Dark

As the novel's title implies, along with puzzles, light and dark are important concepts that Doerr uses in their most traditional sense. Light is associated with goodness and darkness with its opposite.

Doerr is careful to explain that Marie-Laure's world is not a dark one. Though blind, she is still a creature of light. Her other senses, compensating for her blindness, explode into a whorl of colors, sounds and feelings. Her father, who is all things to her, is also all the colors, changing like a kaleidoscope to match what he is doing at the moment, such as red when he is cooking and blue when he is happily tinkering at home. In turn, his love for her feels like an explosion of brightness to Daniel. Madame's peaches taste like sunlight, and she says that helping the resistance has put the light back in her eyes. Etienne shares in this sentiment, feeling that he can see clearly again when he steps up to help with the resistance. As the radio professors explain to Werner and Jutta, there is no light inside the brain, yet it can construct a world of light. Their theme song for their program appropriately, is "Clair de Lune," which means light of the moon.

Werner longs for the light, the antithesis of the dark world of the mines in which his father died and a life to which he fears he will be condemned. He imagines himself as a scientist carrying a lantern, a beacon against the darkness, to an observatory where he will watch the light of the stars and solve puzzles of science. As he learns about infrared and ultraviolet from his copy of *The Principles of Mechanics*, he feels a world of light opening to him. However, the book is confiscated by a Nazi official because a Jew wrote it, shutting down that source of light for Werner.

As is traditional in so many works about World War II, the Nazis bring darkness. Rumor has it they even carry pills that make instant fog. As they approach Paris, they snuff out radio stations as if they were candles, dousing the light of knowledge that freedom of information brings, and then the whole City of Lights goes dark. Prewar Paris is portrayed as a place of light, beauty, and freedom, especially in Jutta's imaginings, while Berlin is dark and mechanical. When the Germans come to Saint-Malo, even the fireflies leave, but Madame and Etienne's transmitter are portrayed as sparks of remaining light. As Germany reels under the Allied bombing, Werner's school loses electricity, making its darkness even more prominent. Germany is really going dark. When Werner arrives in the east, the day is sunless. Then, as they ride on their killing missions, the young soldiers destroy sunflowers, which is another emblem of light. In contrast, their opposites, the young, liberating American soldiers, are described as bright-eyed, bringing back the light.

At the end, when he is trapped in the cellar in Saint-Malo, Werner is starving in the darkness and thinking of the wrongs he has done. He comes to understand that no darkness is total. There is always a hope of light, yet another illustration of the theme that life will recover and march on, even if not for Werner.

What is Lost

Werner stresses the novel's important point that so much possibility is lost to war. In World War I, Etienne became a victim of post-traumatic stress disorder after seeing his beloved brother, Henri, killed in battle. The LeBlancs, with their knowledge of radio waves and science, were signalmen. Etienne became a recluse after his brother's death, anything his scientific mind might have created or taught lost to the outside world. This is even truer for Werner, who might have gone on to invent many wondrous and useful things. Frederick, with his ability to see truths that no one else wants to admit, must hide his eyeglasses, a symbol of his ability to see, from the teachers and students at Schulpforta. With his love of stars and birds, he too might have gone on to do great things, and certainly would have been a remarkable adult with his great empathy for living things. Instead, he is trapped in his damaged brain after being forced to attend Schulpforta because of his parents' desire to rise to the top of the Nazi pecking order.

Even Volkheimer, the giant of a boy who becomes a killing machine on the eastern front, turns out to have a gentle, music-loving side. He sees through the game the teachers play with the tortured prisoner. He lets Werner get away with not exposing Etienne's transmitter, and he allows Werner to go save Marie-Laure. However, Volkheimer's soul is lost, too. His wartime experiences scar him to the point that he lives out his life as a lonely, haunted TV antenna repairman.

Though they do as they are ordered, Werner senses that all the cadets, even the most vicious bullies, are feeling the same inner anguish. With so many losses among the boys of this generation, it is the brave girls who go on to achieve, both in their careers and as mothers. Despite having lost Werner and being raped by Russian soldiers, Jutta teaches math and has a good marriage. Her little boy is a prodigy who has Werner's love of mechanics, a great potential that she nurtures wisely. Marie-Laure is a professor who has contributed much to the knowledge of snails and has a daughter who is a violinist, bringing music to the world. The teachers at Schulpforta thought they were improving the evolution of humanity, but it is really girls like Jutta and Marie-Laure who do so, taking comfort in starting over with the next generation. That they make so much of their lives, after what they suffered, above all brings home the theme that life does go on .

Author's Style

A terrifying beauty informs the story of Werner and Marie-Laure. Every sentence, paragraph and page is polished like the diamond that von Rumpel seeks, although the horrors of World War II and the Third Reich emerge starkly. One passage, for example, evokes Picasso's classic painting *Guernica*. It is a visual representation of the same theme, depicting a priest scattering holy water on his burning town and horses gone mad, running amid the flames.

By its very nature, this long novel is not an easy read, and its organization is its chief flaw. Though divided into one hundred and seventy-eight short chapters, the story threads often make confusing jumps in time. Sometimes the reader may have to flip back and forth to figure out, for example, how and when Marie-Laure learned that the German intruder had a limp. Another concern is that the great crime against humanity that was the Holocaust comes up only a few times, and only obliquely. Perhaps Anthony Doerr deliberately focuses on stories outside of the Holocaust arc because less focus has been on them, but there is still a feeling of something missing. In addition, the Nazi characters are often treated perfunctorily. The teachers at Werner's school are evil, pure and simple.

The major characters, however, are so well crafted that they all come vibrantly to life, even those who have little time in the spotlight. The storylines are refreshing, too. It is much better for the novel, for example, that Werner and Marie-Laure do not become *Titanic* movie-style lovers, so that they stay real. The depth of the characters beautifully reinforces the novel's ultimate message that, despite all the horrors of war, goodness and love, more than anything else, abide.

~~~~ END OF INSTAREAD ~~~~

Thank you for purchasing this Instaread book

**Download the Instaread mobile app to get
unlimited text & audio summaries
of bestselling books.**

Visit Instaread.co
to learn more.

Lightning Source UK Ltd.
Milton Keynes UK
UKHW020439040919
349126UK00010B/1910/P